HOW TO MIX BEATS

Slime Green Beats

Disclaimer

The info provided in *How to Mix Beats* is for education and information only. The content comes from extensive research and experience by the author, Slime Green Beats. It is meant to help readers improve their music production skills in mixing and mastering.

The author and publisher tried to make sure the book is accurate and complete. Music tech and techniques change fast, so they can't guarantee the info will stay current or work for everyone.

The methods in this book may not work for every user. This is due to differences in skills, music projects, and the ever-changing tech in audio production. Readers are encouraged to think for themselves. They should adjust the advice and techniques in this book to fit their needs and situations.

The author and publisher disclaim any liability. They disclaim it for direct, indirect, incidental, or consequential loss or damage resulting from the use of the information in this book. The purchase and use of this book are done at the reader's own risk.

Any trademarks, service marks, or product names are assumed to be the property of their owners. They are used only for reference. There is no implied endorsement for any of the products or services used in this book.

This disclaimer is part of the book. By reading it, you agree that you are using the information at your own risk. Readers should consult with a professional when necessary and where appropriate.

First paperback edition

ISBN 979-8-9907815-4-2 (paperback)

Table of Contents

Introduction to Beat Mixing and Mastering

Hello, aspiring music producers and beat aficionados! You're about to start a big journey of learning the art and science of beat mixing and mastering. This chapter is your gateway to understanding how these processes make your music better. They ensure your beats sound pro and stand out in the competitive music industry.

This chapter is a foundation for the full exploration of mixing and mastering techniques that will follow. This book is designed for you, whether you're just starting or looking to refine your skills further. We aim to equip you with the knowledge and insights needed to enhance your beats and achieve a polished, industry-standard sound.

The Crucial Distinction: Mixing vs. Mastering

Let's clarify the key difference between mixing and mastering. This is essential for any serious producer. Mixing is the intricate process of blending individual tracks within a session to achieve a harmonious and dynamic whole. It involves adjusting levels and panning. It also involves adding effects like equalization (EQ), compression, and reverb. These steps create a cohesive and engaging sound.

Mastering, on the other hand, is the final step in the music production process, taking your well-mixed track and polishing it and making sure it works on all systems and media. Mastering involves fine-tuning the track's sound. It enhances clarity and ensures consistent loudness. This process prepares the track for release.

Understanding and using good mixing and mastering techniques is key to turning a good beat into a great one. These processes are not just technical needs. They are also chances to make your sound unique. A well-mixed and mastered track shows your professionalism. It reflects your dedication to quality. It impacts how the industry sees your music.

As we delve into the nuances of mixing and mastering, remember that the journey is as important as the destination. The skills you develop here will not only enhance your current projects but also set the stage for your ongoing growth as a music producer. We'll share wisdom from pros. We'll dissect the elements that make beats succeed to keep you motivated and engaged.

As we conclude this introductory chapter, remember that your journey in beat mixing and mastering is a marathon, not a sprint. The principles and techniques we'll explore are your tools for crafting a signature sound that can elevate your music career. With each chapter, we'll delve deeper, building on these foundational concepts and guiding you toward becoming a master of your craft.

Let's start this exciting journey together. We're committed to excellence and love innovation in the world of beat production. Your path to mastering the art of beat mixing and mastering begins now.

Understanding the Role of Mixing and Mastering in Beat Production

This chapter delves into the key roles of mixing and mastering in a music track's lifecycle. It focuses on beats. Mixing and mastering are not just final steps in production. They are crucial processes that bring life to a beat. They ensure it sounds professional and emotional and meets industry standards.

Mixing: The Art of Balance and Creativity

Mixing is where your musical vision starts to take shape in the sonic realm. You balance elements in your track. These are drums, bass, melodies, and vocals. You do this to create a cohesive and engaging sound. But mixing goes beyond just balance. It's about sculpting your beat's sound, boosting its emotion, and ensuring clarity and punch.

- Technical Aspects: We'll explore how to achieve optimal levels, stereo imaging, and frequency distribution, ensuring each element sits perfectly in the mix.

- Creative Decisions: Mixing also involves making creative decisions, like applying effects (reverb, delay, etc.) to enhance the vibe and texture of the beat.

Mastering: The Final Polish

Mastering is the last step in music production. It aims to make sure your beat sounds great on any playback system. It involves critical listening and fine-tuning, which enhances the sound by adjusting for loudness, clarity, and depth. It also ensures the track meets industry standards for release.

- Consistency and Cohesion: Mastering ensures that your beat not only stands alone but also sits well in an album or playlist, maintaining consistency across various tracks.

- Technical Compliance: We'll cover how mastering adjusts the final mix to the technical specifications required for different formats and distribution channels.

The Synergy Between Mixing and Mastering

Understanding the interplay between mixing and mastering is key to producing top-notch beats. Mixing focuses on the elements and their relationships within a track. Mastering takes a global view. It enhances the mix and ensures it works on all systems and formats.

- Collaborative Dynamics: You'll learn about how the mixing engineer and mastering engineer work together, often with the producer, to achieve the desired sonic outcome.

- Creative and Technical Balance: Achieving a balance between the creative aspects of mixing and the technical precision of mastering is crucial for a successful track.

Impact on Beat Production

A well-mixed and mastered beat sounds pro. It also has the power to connect more deeply with the audience. It can stand out in the market and meet the tech requirements for distribution and playback.

Essential Skills for Beat Makers

Understanding mixing and mastering is critical, empowering you, the beat maker, to improve your tracks. These processes are key skills in your toolkit. They let you create beats that sound great and connect with listeners. They also help you succeed in the competitive music industry.

Essential Equipment and Software

To produce beats that resonate with listeners and stand out in the industry, you need the right tools. This chapter guides you through the key equipment and software that are needed for pro mixing and mastering.

Hardware Essentials

- A computer is the heart of your digital audio workstation (DAW). A fast processor and ample RAM are crucial for handling large sessions and plugins.

- An audio interface is the bridge between your analog and digital gear. Look for interfaces with high-quality preamps and converters.

- Monitors and headphones are critical for accurate monitoring. Choose studio monitors. Also, choose headphones that offer a flat frequency response for unbiased listening.

- MIDI (musical instrument digital interface) controllers help you control your DAW. They aid in beat production, mixing, and automation.

- You don't need outboard gear. But compressors, EQs, and effects can add character to digital mixes.

Software Necessities

- A digital audio workstation (DAW) is the core platform for recording, editing, mixing, and mastering. Popular DAWs include Ableton Live, Logic Pro, FL Studio, and Pro Tools. All of these tools are great. We've used FL Studio the most; it is easy for beginners and capable for advanced users as well. We have many tutorials online showing mixing tips and techniques.

- Plugins and virtual instruments can enhance your DAW. They include a range of plugins for EQ, compression, reverb, and delay. They also include virtual instruments for synthesized sounds and samples.

- Analysis tools help ensure your mixes and masters meet industry standards. They include spectrum analyzers, loudness meters, and other diagnostic tools.

Optimizing Your Setup

- Acoustic treatment is essential for creating an accurate listening environment. Treating your room can greatly improve your mixes and masters.

- Ergonomics is about arranging your equipment for comfort and efficiency to reduce fatigue during long sessions.

Software Integration

- Improve your workflow efficiency. Integrate your hardware and software seamlessly to create a workflow that boosts creativity and productivity.
- Updates and upgrades keep your software current, ensuring it works with the latest plugins and features, which improves your production.

Invest in Quality

Having good equipment and software is crucial. They are needed to achieve professional results in mixing and mastering beats. The initial cost might be high. But the right tools will not only improve your work's quality; they will also make your work faster and more enjoyable.

Setting Up Your Mixing and Mastering Workspace

A well-designed workspace is crucial for efficient and effective mixing and mastering. This chapter focuses on creating an environment that fosters creativity and precision to ensure you can produce the best sound.

Ergonomics and Comfort

- Invest in an ergonomic desk and chair to support long hours of work without discomfort.

- Position your studio monitors at ear level. Place them in an equilateral triangle with your listening position. This setup is best for stereo imaging.

- Layout your equipment within easy reach. This will streamline your workflow and reduce strain.

Acoustic Treatment

- Understand how your room's size and shape affect sound. Plan your setup accordingly.
- Use acoustic panels and diffusers. They minimize reflections and manage bass frequencies. This ensures clear and accurate sound.
- Identify and optimize the sweet spot in your room where the sound from the monitors is most accurate.

Monitoring and Reference

- Calibrate your studio monitors for a consistent, flat frequency response.
- Use reference tracks. They are professionally mixed and mastered. Use them as guides for your decisions in setup and in mixing and mastering.

Technical Setup

- Understand the signal path in your studio setup, from the audio source through your interface to your monitors.
- Manage cables to reduce clutter and interference. This ensures a clean and safe workspace.

Optimize Your Digital Workspace

- Set up your DAW for fast work. Use templates, keyboard shortcuts, and custom settings.
- Organize your plugins and virtual instruments for easy access. This will make using them efficient during sessions.

Environmental Considerations

- Choose lighting that is comfortable for long sessions and minimizes eye strain.
- Make sure your workspace has good ventilation. It should be isolated from outside noise for uninterrupted work. It is also recommended that

you keep distractions away, such as your phone or having a TV on.

A Conducive Space for Creativity

Creating a good workspace for mixing and mastering is about more than just the setup. It's about crafting an environment that inspires creativity. It must also allow for the precision needed in music production. Pay attention to ergonomics, acoustics, monitoring, and your digital workflow. Your aim is to build a space that boosts your productivity and the quality of your beats.

Understanding Levels, Balance, and Panning

The key to a great mix is managing levels, balance, and panning. This chapter guides you through practical techniques and examples to optimize these critical aspects, which ensure that each part of your beat is clear and adds to the sound.

Managing Levels: Setting the Stage for Clarity

Managing levels starts with gain staging, which makes sure each track is set to an optimal level before adding effects or processing. This avoids clipping and maintains the quality of the audio.

Example: Begin by setting the level of your kick drum, which typically drives the track. Aim for a peak level around -12 dB on your meter. Then adjust the levels of other elements like the bass, snare, and hi-hats relative to the kick. Make sure each element is distinct but not too loud.

Balancing Frequencies for Cohesion

A balanced mix needs careful adjustment. You must adjust the frequency of each track. This ensures that all elements combine well. No one frequency range should dominate.

Example: Use an EQ to roll off the low end on non-bass elements to prevent muddiness. For instance, a high-pass filter at around 100 Hz on guitar and vocal tracks can help clean up the mix, allowing the bass and kick drum to dominate the lower frequencies.

Panning: Creating a Three-Dimensional Soundscape

Panning lets you place elements in the stereo field, not just to avoid clashes but also to make a lifelike and immersive listening experience.

Example: To create a balanced stereo image, pan your main rhythm elements like the kick and bass to the center, as they form the backbone of your track. Place snare slightly off-center to add dimension. Place guitars and keyboards apart. This makes space seem bigger. For instance, if you pan a rhythm guitar 30% to the left, consider panning a keyboard layer 30% to the right.

Using Automation for Dynamic Mixing

Automation is a powerful tool. It can adjust levels and panning throughout the track. This enhances the emotional impact and keeps listeners interested.

Example: Automate the panning of a lead guitar to move across the stereo field during a solo, starting from the left and slowly moving to the right, which can draw the listener's attention and add excitement. Do the same for background vocals. Increase the volume during the chorus. Then decrease it during verses. This adds depth and impact when needed.

Monitoring Levels Across Various Systems

Check your mix often. Listen at different volumes and on various systems. This will ensure balance and compatibility and that your mix sounds good through headphones, car speakers, and a club sound system.

Example: After setting levels on your studio monitors, listen to your mix on consumer headphones and in your car. Make notes of any unbalanced elements. Then adjust levels or EQ settings to ensure consistent sound across all devices.

Mastery Through Practice

Understanding levels, balance, and panning is essential. These are key skills for any mixer. These practical techniques and examples will help you make smart decisions, which will improve the clarity, depth, and dynamics of your mixes. Practice regularly and listen critically to hone these skills and develop your unique mixing style.

Equalization Techniques for Beats

Equalization (EQ) is a powerful tool in mixing that allows you to shape and enhance the sound of each track. It can make your beats punchier and clearer by adjusting frequency ranges to boost or cut specific elements. This chapter provides practical examples and techniques to help you use EQ well in your mixes.

Understanding the Frequency Spectrum

Before using EQ, you must understand the frequency spectrum. You must also understand how different frequencies affect the sound of instruments.

Example: Low frequencies (20 Hz to 250 Hz) add depth and power, which are crucial for elements like kick drums and basslines. Mid frequencies (250 Hz to 2 kHz) contribute to the warmth and presence of guitars, vocals, and pianos. High frequencies (2 kHz to 20 kHz) bring clarity and sparkle to cymbals and hi-hats. They also add air to vocal tracks.

EQ Techniques for Beat Elements

Each part of your beat may need different EQ settings, based on its role and the desired effect.

- Kick Drum EQ: To make the kick drum thump and stand out in the mix, boost around 80–100 Hz for low-end power and cut around 300–400 Hz to reduce muddiness. A slight boost around 3–5 kHz can enhance the kick's attack.

- Snare Drum EQ: Enhance the body of the snare by boosting around 200 Hz. To bring out the snap, boost slightly around 5 kHz. If the snare sounds too harsh, apply a slight cut around 8 kHz.

- Bass EQ: Roll off the extreme low end below 40 Hz to clean up unnecessary rumble. Boosting around 60–80 Hz can add warmth. To make the bass cut through the mix, consider a boost around 700 Hz–1 kHz.

- Vocal EQ: Apply a high-pass filter up to 80–100 Hz to eliminate low-frequency noise. Boost slightly around 2–4 kHz for clarity and presence, and if needed, add a gentle boost around 10–12 kHz for brightness.

Corrective vs. Creative EQ

Understanding when to use EQ to correct issues versus when to use it creatively is crucial for achieving a professional mix.

- Corrective EQ fixes sound problems. It removes muddiness from a guitar by cutting 200–300 Hz. It reduces vocal sibilance by cutting harsh highs.

- Creative EQ involves making stylistic EQ choices to enhance sound character, for example, by adding a dramatic high-frequency boost to a synth lead to make it sparkle or enhancing the low end on a drum bus for added power.

Utilizing EQ in Context

Always consider how the EQ adjustments affect the mix as a whole. It's important to frequently toggle the EQ on and off to evaluate whether the changes improve the overall sound.

Example: When adjusting the EQ on a bass track, listen not only as a solo but also in context with the kick drum and the rest of the rhythm section to ensure they work harmoniously without clashing.

EQ as a Mix Sculpting Tool

Using EQ well is about balance and intention. You need to know what each track needs for it to best contribute to the mix. Through the examples and techniques in this chapter, you are now better equipped to make informed EQ decisions. These decisions will raise the quality of your beats. Practice consistently, and use your ears critically to develop a keen sense for how EQ can transform your mixes.

Dynamics Processing: Compression and Limiting

Dynamics processing includes compression and limiting. It is key for controlling the energy and volume of your beats. It ensures they sound polished and impactful. This chapter provides practical examples. It also gives techniques for using these tools well in your mixes.

Understanding Compression

Compression reduces the dynamic range of an audio signal. It makes the loud parts quieter and the quiet parts louder. This can glue the mix together and add punch.

- Drum Compression: To add punch to a drum track, set a moderate to fast attack to clamp down on the initial hit quickly, and a medium release so the compressor recovers before the next hit. A ratio of 4:1 is a good starting point. This setting enhances the impact while keeping the drums feeling natural.

- Vocal Compression: For vocals, use a slower attack time to let some of the initial dynamics through and a faster release to maintain naturalness. A ratio between 2:1 and 3:1 usually works well, helping to keep the vocal performance consistent in the mix.

Applying Limiting

Limiting is a type of compression with a high ratio. It is used mainly to stop audio peaks from exceeding a level. This ensures the mix doesn't clip and stays within a loudness range.

- Master Bus Limiting: When applying limiting on the master bus, aim for a threshold that just catches the peaks, with a fast attack and a release time that complements the tempo of the track. This will maximize loudness without causing noticeable pumping or distortion.

Techniques for Dynamics Control

- Parallel compression, also known as New York compression, involves mixing a dry (unprocessed) signal with a compressed version of itself. This technique is often used on drums. It blends in some compressed signal with the original. It maintains dynamic range while making the drums seem louder and more energetic.
    - Example: Set up a send from the drum track to an auxiliary track with a compressor set for heavy compression. Mix this heavily compressed signal back in with the original. Do this until you get the desired punch without losing the natural dynamics.

- Side-chain compression uses the audio signal from one track to trigger the compressor on another, commonly used to make space in the mix, such as having the bass duck when the kick hits.

- Example: Apply a compressor to the bass track and set the kick drum as the side-chain input. Set the compressor to react quickly with a fast attack and a medium release. This will make the bass briefly quieter every time the kick hits, to make room for the kick.

Best Practices for Dynamics Processing

- Before applying compression or limiting, make sure each track is properly gain staged to prevent clipping and ensure the processor works efficiently.

- Always listen to the effects of compression and limiting within the context of the full mix, not just solo tracks. This approach ensures that adjustments contribute positively to the overall sound.

Dynamics as a Creative and Technical Tool

Using dynamics processing well can greatly improve the quality and impact of your beats. By understanding and using the techniques in this chapter, you can use compression and limiting as creative forces, not just fixes, in your mixing tools.

Adding Depth and Space with Reverb and Delay

Reverb and delay are crucial effects for adding depth, space, and dimension to your mixes. They help elements sit better in the mix. They create a sense of space and can even add emotion to your music. This chapter will give examples and techniques to help you master these effects and use their full potential in your projects.

Reverb: Crafting Atmospheric Depth

Reverb simulates sounds' natural reflections off surfaces. It adds a sense of space and ambiance.

- Vocal Reverb: To add depth to vocals without muddying the mix, use a plate reverb with a moderate decay time of around 1.2 seconds. Cut the low frequencies on the reverb to prevent muddiness. Boost a bit at 5 kHz to add clarity.

- Drum Room Reverb: To give drums a sense of space as if they were recorded in a live room, use a room reverb with a shorter decay time of about 0.8 seconds. Increase the pre-delay to about 30 ms. This adds depth and keeps the reverb from smearing the first drum hits.

Delay: Echoes That Enhance Rhythm

Delay repeats the incoming audio at set intervals. This creates a rhythmic echo effect. It can add movement and excitement to a track.

- Guitar Delay: For a rhythmic guitar part, apply a dotted eighth-note delay to create a cascading echo effect. Use a feedback setting of about 30% to keep the effect discrete but perceptible, adding rhythmic complexity.

- Synth Pad Delay: Apply a stereo ping-pong delay to a synth pad to enhance its atmospheric quality. Set the delay to a quarter-note on one side and an eighth-note on the other, with a low feedback setting to keep the effect subtle.

Combining Reverb and Delay

Using reverb and delay together can be powerful but requires careful balancing to avoid a cluttered or washed-out mix.

Example: On lead vocals, apply a light reverb to add space and a slapback delay with a single repeat to enhance presence. The key is to ensure that the delay and reverb do not compete. You do this by adjusting the levels. The goal is to make the reverb more prominent in the mix. The delay should provide a subtle thickening effect.

Advanced Spatial Effects

Experiment with advanced techniques to manipulate space and depth in more sophisticated ways.

- Modulated Reverb and Delay: Apply modulation to the tail of a reverb or the feedback path of a delay to add texture and movement. This can be particularly effective on static sounds, giving them life and making them more engaging.

- Automated Spatial Effects: Automate the wet/dry mix of reverb and delay or their decay and feedback parameters throughout a track to create dynamic changes in the soundstage. For example, add reverb during a chorus to make it expansive. Then reduce it in the verse to bring the vocals forward.

Mastery of Space and Time

Understanding and using reverb and delay well are key skills. They are needed by any mixer who wants to craft pro, emotional music. These effects not only add depth and space but also help to glue the mix together when used thoughtfully. By practicing the techniques outlined in this chapter, you can add a new dimension to your mixes and achieve a more polished, dynamic sound.

Creative Effects and Processing Techniques

Creative effects and processing techniques go beyond basic mixing tools. They offer unique ways to shape sound. And to manipulate it. This chapter covers many new effects that can turn a simple mix into a captivating sound. It includes practical examples to guide your experimentation.

Saturation and Distortion

Saturation and distortion can add warmth, grit, or edge to your sounds. They enhance the sounds' presence and character.

- Warmth in Vocals: Gently apply a tube saturation plugin on a vocal track to add warmth and body. Set the drive around 20–30% and blend it until the vocals sound richer without becoming overly distorted.

- Distorted Guitar: For rock or metal tracks, use a guitar amp simulator or a distortion pedal plugin to add crunch and sustain to electric guitar parts. Try different pedal settings and amp models to find the perfect tone. It should match the song's energy.

Modulation Effects

Chorus, flanger, phaser, and tremolo are modulation effects. They can add depth, movement, or psychedelic flavors to your mix.

- Chorus on Synths: Add a chorus effect to a synth pad to thicken the sound and add movement. Adjust the rate and depth to taste, ensuring the effect enhances the pad without overwhelming it.

- Flanger on Drums: Applying a flanger to a drum bus can create a sweeping, dynamic texture. Use a slow rate and moderate depth to prevent the effect from dominating the drums while still adding a subtle rhythmic variation.

Pitch and Time Manipulation

Changing pitch and time can greatly alter a sound, making the sound more flexible and interesting.

- Vocal Pitch Correction: Use a pitch correction tool on vocals to tweak the melody or create harmonies. Set the retune speed for a natural sound or a robotic effect, depending on the desired outcome.

- Time-Stretching Beats: Apply time-stretching to drum loops to match them to your track's tempo without changing the pitch. Use high-quality algorithms to maintain the clarity and punch of the drums.

Granular Synthesis

Granular synthesis breaks sound into small grains and then resynthesizes them to create new textures.

- Atmospheric Pads: Turn a simple recorded sound, like a note from a piano or a bell, into a complex, evolving pad by manipulating the grain size, density, and playback position.

Creative Dynamic Processing

You can use dynamic effects, like side-chain compression and gating, creatively. They shape the rhythm and dynamics of your mix.

- Side-chain Compression on Bass: Use side-chain compression to duck the bass line whenever the kick drum hits. This creates a pumping effect that is popular in electronic and dance music.

- Gated Reverb on Snare: Apply a gated reverb to a snare drum to achieve an '80s pop snare sound. Adjust the gate's threshold and decay to control how abruptly the reverb cuts off.

Unleashing Creative Potential

The use of creative effects is about exploration and pushing boundaries. Each effect offers many sonic options that can transform boring tracks into memorable creations. You can enhance the art of your mixes by using the techniques shown in the examples. Remember, the key to using effects creatively is by always experimenting and fine-tuning to fit the context of your music.

Advanced Mixing Techniques for Beats

Advanced mixing involves more than just balancing levels and basic effects. It requires a deep understanding of sound manipulation and creative processing to truly enhance your music. This chapter covers advanced methods that can turn a good mix into a pro-sounding production and includes examples to guide you.

Parallel Compression: Achieving Punch and Clarity

Parallel compression is also called New York compression. It is a type of dynamic range compression. It is used to mix an uncompressed signal with a compressed version of itself.

Example on Drums: Send your drum tracks to an auxiliary bus and apply heavy compression with a low threshold and high ratio. Adjust the attack to fast to catch the transients and a medium release to maintain natural decay. Mix this heavily compressed signal back with the original uncompressed drums. The result is powerful, punchy drums that still retain their dynamic feel.

Stereo Enhancement: Widening Your Mix

Making the stereo image wider can make your mix sound bigger without crowding the center.

Example with Synth Pads: Apply a stereo widener to a synth pad and adjust the width to subtly increase its spread across the stereo field. Be cautious of over-widening, which can lead to phase issues when played back in mono.

Advanced EQ Techniques: Surgical and Musical EQ

Using EQ to fix issues and improve music is a key skill in advanced mixing.

- Surgical EQ on Vocals: Identify any harsh resonant peaks in vocal tracks using a narrow EQ and reduce them slightly to smooth out the sound.
- EQ for Bass: Add a broad boost at 60 Hz to warm the bass. Also, add a slight boost at 2 kHz to bring out the string pluck. This will make the bass more present in the mix.

Dynamic EQ: Responsive Frequency Adjustment

Dynamic EQ applies EQ changes only when certain thresholds are met. It combines the precision of EQ with the responsiveness of dynamics.

Example on a Dynamic Vocal Track: Use dynamic EQ to reduce sibilance only when it becomes excessive by setting a high-frequency band to trigger reduction at high levels. This keeps the vocals clear. It doesn't dim the rest.

Creative Use of Effects: Delays and Reverbs

Delays and reverbs are not just for adding echo or ambiance. They can be used creatively for rhythm and space.

- Rhythmic Delay on Guitar: Set a delay with a dotted eighth-note timing on a rhythm guitar to create a complex, interlocking pattern with the original signal.
- Pre-delay on Reverb for Vocals: Increase the pre-delay setting on a vocal reverb to around 80–120 ms. This separates the vocals from the reverb tail, enhancing clarity and making the reverb effect more pronounced without clouding the vocals.

Automation for Dynamic Mixing

Automation allows for changes. It provides a dynamic evolution to the mix.

- Automating Filter Sweeps on Synths: Automate a low-pass filter from high to low during a breakdown section to create a sweeping effect that increases tension, then open it back up for the drop to release the energy.

Mastering the Mix

Advanced mixing techniques can dramatically improve the quality and impact of your music. By mastering these techniques, you will improve your technical skills. You will also deepen your creative expression. Use these as a starting point. Then adapt them to fit your style and each project's needs.

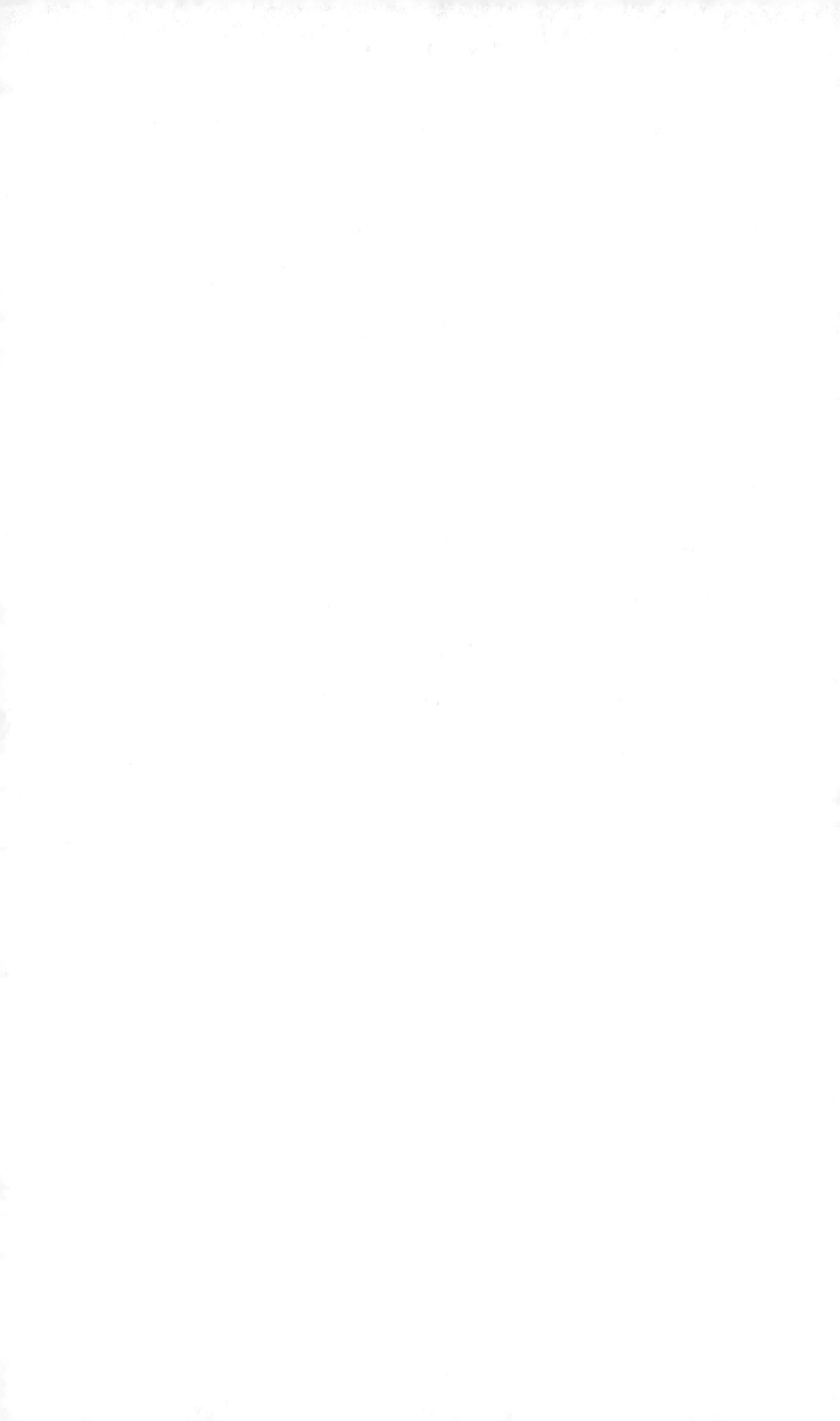

Preparing Your Mix for Mastering

As you approach the final stages of making a beat, preparing your mix for mastering is crucial. It should be handled with care and precision. This chapter covers fine-tuning your mix. It ensures it's ready for mastering, which is where the final changes to bring your music to commercial quality will be made.

Understanding the Importance of Headroom

Headroom is essential in a mix to prevent clipping and allow the mastering engineer room to work. A proper mix has headroom for peaks at -6 dB to -3 dB. This range ensures space for mastering to boost loudness and dynamics without distortion.

The Role of the Stereo Bus

In the mixing phase, it's tempting to add effects like compression or EQ to the stereo bus. This is done to make the mix sound finished. However, these should be used sparingly or avoided in the pre-mastering stage. The engineer will make broad enhancements to the whole track, and pre-applied effects can limit their ability to make the needed adjustments.

Balancing the Mix Elements

The balance of elements within your mix is critical. The mix should fit together well. Each element should sit well in the overall soundstage, ensuring nothing is too loud or lost. This balance is not just about volume but also about frequency and space. Each part's placement affects the mix's clarity and depth.

Ensuring Consistency Across Tracks

If you're preparing an album or an EP, consistency across tracks becomes paramount. The tonal balance, dynamic range, and overall loudness should feel cohesive from one track to the next. This helps maintain the listener's interest. It also conveys the intended narrative or emotion of the whole body of work.

Technical Preparation

The technical aspect of preparing your mix for mastering involves exporting your tracks in the correct format. Typically, this means a high-resolution audio file, like a 24-bit WAV or AIFF file, with no dithering applied. The sampling rate should match the project's original settings. This will avoid unnecessary sample rate conversion.

Communication with Your Mastering Engineer

Finally, effective communication with your mastering engineer is crucial. Providing notes about your vision for the track will help as will any concerns you have and the intended formats for distribution. This will help the mastering engineer tailor their approach to meet your goals. It will ensure the final product meets your expectations.

Attention to Detail

Preparing your mix for mastering is about ensuring that the track is in the best possible state to undergo the final enhancements. It's a phase where attention to detail and a critical ear play significant roles in bridging the gap between a good mix and a great master. By carefully following these steps, you are setting the stage for the mastering process, which will improve and refine your music so it resonates with your audience and meets industry standards.

Introduction to Mastering

Mastering is the last step in music production. It adds the final artistic and technical touches to a mix. These touches ensure the mix sounds good on all playback systems and media. This chapter introduces the basics of mastering. It sets the stage for understanding how this phase shapes your music's final sound.

The Goal of Mastering

Mastering creates a cohesive listening experience for an album or single. It ensures each track is balanced and matches the others. It's not just about making music louder. It's about refining the sound, making it clearer, and meeting industry standards for release.

The Mastering Signal Chain

A typical mastering signal chain has many high-quality audio tools. These include equalization, compression, limiting, and stereo enhancement. Each tool serves a specific purpose. They balance the frequency spectrum and achieve the desired loudness and dynamic range.

The Process of Mastering

Mastering starts with critical listening to find sonic issues that need fixing. This could involve making small changes to the EQ to balance the mix's tones. Or it could mean using compression to control dynamics to make the music hit harder. Then limiting is applied to make the track louder, which prevents clipping and keeps dynamics.

Mastering also has technical aspects. These include setting the right levels for digital distribution, ensuring the track meets the loudness standards of streaming platforms, and making a final master that is free from distortion and other unwanted artifacts.

Preparing for Different Formats

Mastering can vary depending on the final distribution format. For example, mastering for vinyl has different considerations than for digital streaming. It requires attention to low-frequency control and the stereo image. Understanding these nuances is crucial to ensure the best possible sound quality across all formats.

The Role of a Mastering Engineer

Modern technology has made mastering more accessible. But the role of a skilled mastering engineer is crucial. They bring an objective ear and special expertise to the process. They often catch subtle nuances that can make or break the final product.

Mastering is both an art and a science. It needs a deep understanding of sound, a critical ear, and special tools and techniques. Mastering is a journey of subtlety and refinement. The goal is to deliver a final product that stands out in today's competitive music world.

Mastering Tools and Equipment

Mastering puts the final polish on your music, ensuring it's ready for public consumption. This chapter covers the tools and gear needed for mastering. It gives insight into how they are used to achieve a balanced, cohesive, and commercially viable final product.

Mastering in the Modern Studio

The modern mastering studio has both state-of-the-art digital tools and traditional analog equipment. It offers the best of both worlds. The choice is between analog and digital. It depends on the project's needs, the music's genre, and the mastering engineer's preference.

Digital Audio Workstation (DAW)

In mastering, the DAW is more than a playback system. It's a place for precise edits, sonic improvements, and adding metadata. High-resolution audio support and a clean, intuitive workflow are crucial for effective mastering in a DAW.

Analog Gear

Analog equipment remains a staple in mastering for its warmth and character. Key pieces include the following:

- Analog EQs offer hands-on control. They have the unique tone-shaping abilities of hardware.
- Hardware compressors and limiters are revered for their dynamic control. They can add a distinctive sound.

Digital Tools

Digital mastering tools offer precision and recall capabilities unmatched by analog gear.

- Plugins are high-quality. They copy the nuances of analog gear. They also add the benefits of total recall and flexibility.
- Digital processors are specialized for mastering. They provide surgical EQ, dynamics control, and stereo imaging.

Monitoring System

Accurate monitoring is paramount in mastering. Mastering-grade speakers and headphones have flat frequency response. They offer detailed sound representation. This enables critical listening decisions. These decisions translate well across various playback systems.

Outboard Effects and Processors

Mastering focuses on EQ and dynamics control. But you can use outboard effects. These include harmonic exciters, stereo enhancers, and specialized filters. Use them sparingly. They add the final touches to a track.

Mastering for Various Formats

Mastering equipment and tools must also cater to the various distribution formats:

- Vinyl mastering requires special EQ and dynamics. You need them for pressing.
- CD and digital: You need high-resolution digital masters. Pay careful attention to bit depth and sampling rates.
- To optimize playback, you must consider loudness normalization for different streaming platforms.

Mastering tools and equipment are crucial in transforming a good mix into a great master. Mastering engineers can opt for the tactile feel of analog gear or the precision of digital tools. They need a deep understanding of their equipment to make the final product shine. We've aimed to give you the knowledge to appreciate the nuances of mastering equipment.

Mastering EQ and Compression

Mastering EQ and compression are crucial in mastering. Each plays a pivotal role in improving a track's sound. This chapter is about the careful use of these tools. They are to make your music sound polished on all playback systems.

Mastering EQ: The Art of Balance

In mastering, EQ is used to fine-tune the tonal balance of a mix. It addresses any frequency imbalances overlooked during mixing. *Mixing* EQ may be drastic and focused on individual instruments. In contrast, *mastering* EQ adjustments are subtle and affect the entire track.

- Mastering EQ involves broad, gentle boosts and cuts that enhance or reduce frequencies gently. This ensures the track sounds balanced and cohesive.

- Mastering finds areas needing corrective EQ to remove muddiness, harshness, or imbalance. Also, mastering finds areas where a boost can enhance clarity, warmth, or presence.

- In mastering, EQ decisions are made while continuously referencing other tracks. This ensures the sound meets industry standards.

Mastering Compression: Dynamic Control

Compression in mastering is about controlling the dynamic range. It makes the track sound cohesive and ensures it competes in loudness and energy in commercial music.

- Unlike mixing, where compression can be aggressive on elements, mastering compression is subtle. It's used to glue the mix and boost consistency.

- Understanding the difference between peak and RMS (root mean square) is vital, affecting how the compressor responds to the track's dynamics.

- Compression in mastering involves considering the stereo image. The beat needs to ensure that compression does not hurt the width and depth of the mix.

The Synergy of EQ and Compression

In mastering, EQ and compression work together synergistically. EQ adjustments can change the way a compressor reacts to the signal, and vice versa. It's crucial to switch between these two processes. Refine the settings until the track has a balance of clarity, warmth, punch, and loudness.

- EQ first to balance frequencies. Then compress to control dynamics. Then EQ again to fine-tune after compression.

- Modern mastering tools sometimes combine EQ and compression into one interface. This allows for simultaneous adjustments and more integrated processing choices.

Practical Tips for Effective Mastering

- In mastering, the adage "less is more" holds true. Subtle shifts can have a profound impact on the overall sound, and over-processing can degrade the mix's quality.
- Monitoring at lower levels can reveal balance issues and help prevent ear fatigue, ensuring more consistent and reliable decision-making.

The Final Touch

Mastering EQ and compression are about adding the final touch. They change a good mix into a great master. We've provided the knowledge and tools to let you approach these processes with the skill and precision needed for pro mastering. These skills will ensure your tracks stand up to scrutiny in any listening environment.

Stereo Imaging and Widening Techniques

Stereo imaging and widening techniques are crucial in mastering. They make a mix seem wider and deeper, creating a more immersive listening experience. This chapter explores the methods and tools used to manipulate the stereo field well to ensure your tracks have the space and depth that captivate listeners.

The Essence of Stereo Imaging

Stereo imaging is about managing the space of sound. It determines how wide or narrow the mix seems to the listener. Using stereo imaging well can make a mix feel expansive and airy. It provides space around each element.

Techniques for Stereo Enhancement

- Mid-side processing is a technique that allows separate control over the middle and side of a mix. The middle is the center and the side is the left and right. Improving the side components can widen the sound. It won't affect the mono compatibility.

- Stereo widening plugins are tools for stereo widening. They can enhance the spatial image. But use them carefully to avoid phase issues and ensure mono compatibility.

- The Haas effect is a psychoacoustic phenomenon. Slight delays between left and right channels can create a perception of stereo width. This adds depth and space to the mix.

Balancing Width with Cohesion

While it's tempting to push for the widest possible sound, maintaining balance is key. Over-widening can lead to a mix that feels disjointed or loses its impact on mono playback systems. The goal is to enhance the stereo field while preserving the mix's integrity and balance.

- Listen critically. Always evaluate the stereo width and its impact on the mix's feel. Use both stereo and mono playback to check for phase issues and ensure compatibility.

- Reference tracks can help. They let you compare your work to well-mastered tracks in similar genres. They can help you gauge the right level of stereo enhancement.

Advanced Spatial Techniques

- Ambience and Reverb Tails: Adjusting the reverb in the side channels can add to the sense of space without cluttering the middle of the mix, where vocals and key instruments usually are.

- Dynamic stereo imaging automates the width during different sections of the track. This adds interest and emphasizes moments like a chorus or bridge.

Crafting Immersive Experiences

Stereo imaging and widening are not just technical processes. They are artistic ones. They greatly add to the emotion of a track. By using these techniques well, you can turn a flat mix into a 3D sound, which will engage and move the listener. We've provide the insights and methods needed to master stereo imaging to ensure your tracks are not only heard but also felt in their full spatial glory.

Adding Depth and Dynamics in Mastering

In mastering, the goal is to improve the sound of a mix. This makes it sound good on all playback systems. This chapter addresses mastering techniques that add depth and dynamics to ensure the final product engages the listener and stands out in the music market.

Enhancing Depth in Mastering

In audio, depth is the sense of space and dimensionality. Different elements seem to occupy distinct layers. Achieving this involves careful manipulation of frequency, dynamics, and stereo imaging.

- EQ Layering: Small EQ changes can separate elements in the mix. This gives each its own space and adds depth. For example, adding a little to the high frequencies can make the vocals feel closer. Also, a slight boost in the lows can add depth to the rhythm section.
- Reverb and Ambience: Reverb is added during mixing. But a mastering engineer might add a light touch of reverb or ambience. This glues the mix and adds space without washing out the track. This can work for both drums and melodies.

Dynamics in Mastering

Dynamics in mastering involve the range between the loudest and quietest parts of a track. The aim is to retain the natural dynamics of the performance while ensuring the overall level is competitive and consistent.

- Multiband compression allows dynamic control over specific frequency ranges without affecting the entire mix. It helps to keep or improve the track's dynamic interest.

- Sophisticated limiting can increase loudness while keeping the punch and clarity of the mix. The key is to find the right balance where the track is loud and impactful but not squashed or lifeless.

Achieving Dynamic Range

Dynamic range is crucial for maintaining the emotional impact of music. In mastering, make sure the dynamic range is right for the genre and listening environment.

- Dynamic range measurement tools can help. They ensure that the music keeps enough loudness variety to keep the listener engaged.

- Different genres have different norms for dynamic range. For example, classical music typically has a wide dynamic range, while pop and rock are more compressed.

Techniques for a Dynamic Master

- Parallel Processing: Mixing the raw (dry) signal with the processed (wet) signal can boost the dynamics, adding life and energy back into the track. Heavy processing may have taken these away.
- Volume Automation: You can adjust the volume manually in parts of the track. This preserves or boosts dynamic shifts and makes sure that key moments stand out.

The Art of Dynamic Mastering

Mastering is the final opportunity to ensure that a track is not only technically sound but also emotionally compelling. A mastering engineer can elevate a mix by skillfully adding depth and dynamics. This makes the master resonate with the listener and work well on all platforms. The goal is to achieve a master that feels alive, dynamic, and full of the depth that invites listeners into the music.

Loudness and Level Matching

Loudness and level matching are key in mastering. They make sure your music matches other commercial releases and gives a consistent listening experience across tracks and platforms. This chapter covers the techniques and standards for achieving optimal loudness, ensuring your tracks are competitive and keep their dynamics.

Understanding Loudness Standards

Loudness in audio production is measured in units called LUFS (loudness units full scale), which provide a more consistent measure of perceived loudness than peak or RMS meters. You must learn loudness standards, like those set by the EBU R128 or the ITU-R BS.1770, which are crucial for meeting broadcast and streaming requirements.

The Role of Loudness in Mastering

In mastering, the goal is to achieve a balance between loudness and dynamic range. Too loud, and the music loses its dynamic impact; too quiet, and it fails to capture the listener's attention or compete with other tracks.

- Dynamic Range and Loudness: Keeping a good dynamic range is key. But you must also meet loudness targets. This involves careful use of compression and limiting to increase loudness without crushing the life out of the music.

- Loudness normalization is a new feature on streaming platforms. Achieving a loud master is now less about hitting maximum levels and more about ensuring consistent loudness across tracks and albums.

Techniques for Level Matching

Matching levels is key when comparing tracks or versions of a mix, letting you make informed choices about EQ, compression, and other processing.

- Reference tracks can help. They are professionally mastered and serve as references for loudness and tonal balance. They help ensure your track is competitive in today's music.

- A/B testing is critical. It uses level-matched tracks to reveal subtle differences, guiding mastering to ensure the final product is both polished and dynamic.

Practical Applications

Getting the right loudness level takes technical know-how. It also takes critical listening.

- Use advanced metering tools. They offer LUFS readings, dynamic range indicators, and true peak meters. They help you make informed decisions about loudness and dynamics.

- Understand the factors that affect loudness perception. These factors include frequency and exposure duration. They will help you make better mastering decisions.

Striking the Perfect Balance

Mastering loudness and level matching is about balancing loudness and dynamics. It's about being competitive while keeping range intact. It ensures that your tracks are not only consistent and competitive but that they also deliver the intended emotional and sonic impact.

Mastering for Different Formats and Platforms

Mastering for different formats and platforms is crucial. It ensures your music sounds its best, no matter where and how it's played. This chapter delves into the nuances of mastering for different mediums—from vinyl and CD to digital streaming—and highlights the technical tips and best practices for each.

Vinyl Mastering: The Analog Art

Mastering for vinyl requires special attention. This is due to the limits and traits of the medium. The analog warmth and unique sound of vinyl are highly sought after, but there are constraints to consider:

- Low-end audio can cause needle skipping and distortion. This happens with too much bass or low-end sound. It's important to manage low frequencies and possibly mono them below a certain threshold.

- Vinyl has a limited dynamic range compared to digital formats and needs careful dynamic processing to ensure the recording stays within the medium's limits.

- The length of each side of a vinyl record affects the available dynamic range and frequency response. Longer sides require lower overall levels and high-frequency reduction.

CD Mastering: The Digital Precursor

CDs have more dynamic range and frequency response than vinyl. But they still have their own mastering requirements:

- Adherence to the Red Book standard is critical, which specifies a 44.1 kHz sampling rate and 16-bit depth.

- Peak and RMS levels must be optimized for CD. This makes the audio loud enough without being overly compressed or distorted.

Digital Platforms: The Streaming Era

Mastering for streaming platforms, such as Spotify, Apple Music, and YouTube, has unique challenges. But it also has opportunities:

- Most streaming services use loudness normalization, which adjusts all songs to a consistent volume. You must understand the target loudness levels. They are measured in LUFS for each platform.

- Streaming platforms favor dynamic range over loudness. Unlike the loudness wars of the past, this means music can have more dynamics and less compression.

- Different platforms encode audio in different file formats (e.g., AAC, OGG, MP3). Master to minimize artifacts and keep quality high.

Cross-Platform Consistency

Creating a great master requires balance. It must sound good on all formats and platforms. This needs both technical skill and creative judgment.

Test your masters on different playback systems and platforms often. This will ensure they translate well to different places.

Sometimes making slightly different masters for specific formats or platforms helps. This lets you optimize the master for each medium's traits.

Mastering in the Multi-platform World

Mastering for today's varied listening environments requires being mindful. You have to be aware of the quirks of each format and platform. This includes their technical and perceptual aspects. Tailor your mastering approach for these variations to ensure your music keeps its impact and quality whether it's streamed online, played on the radio, or pressed on vinyl.

The Art of Sequencing and Album Mastering

Sequencing and album mastering are key. They create a cohesive sound and guide the listener on a journey. This chapter focuses on arranging tracks in a meaningful order. It also covers mastering them to form a unified album.

Sequencing: More than Track Order

Sequencing is the strategic ordering of tracks. It enhances the listening experience by considering the ebb and flow of energy, emotion, and themes.

- The flow between songs is as crucial as the individual tracks. Consider the tempo, key, and mood of each track to create a seamless transition.

- Paying attention to story and themes can make an album more engaging and memorable, giving listeners a deeper connection to the music.

Transition Techniques

- Crossfades and interludes can smooth transitions between tracks. They keep the listener engaged throughout the album.

- Silence or a pause between tracks can be a powerful tool, giving the listener space to absorb and anticipate what's next.

Album Mastering: Unity in Diversity

Album mastering ensures consistent sound quality, volume, and tonal balance across all tracks while respecting each song's unique character.

- Consistent loudness levels are essential for a unified listening experience. However, it's important to preserve the dynamic range and not sacrifice the music's emotional impact for loudness.

- Adjust tonal balance to make the album sound cohesive on different playback systems to give a consistent listening experience from start to finish.

The Final Polish

- Mastering is the final polish that can make an album not just a collection of individual tracks but a complete, unified work of art.

- Consideration of the medium (vinyl, CD, digital) is crucial in the final mastering phase, as each has its requirements and nuances.

The Album as a Story

Sequencing and album mastering require more than just precision. They are about storytelling. By arranging and mastering tracks well, you create an album that offers a compelling story. This enhances the listener's experience and emotional connection to the music. These insights and techniques will help you master this art to ensure your albums are not just heard but also felt and remembered.

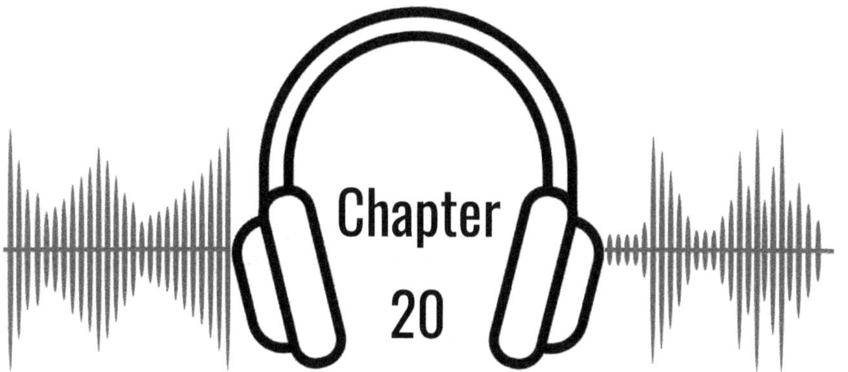

Collaboration and Communication in Mixing and Mastering

Collaboration and communication are vital in mixing and mastering. They often make the difference between a good track and a great one. This chapter explores working with others. They may be artists, producers, or engineers.

Building a Collaborative Environment

Creating a space where all parties feel heard and valued is crucial for a successful collaboration. This involves the following:

- Establish clear roles and duties to ensure all know what is expected of them. They can then focus on their strengths.

- Encourage open dialogue and constructive feedback. This allows for a free exchange of ideas and suggestions to enhance the project.

Communication Strategies

Good communication is key. It ensures everyone's vision is in alignment for the project and the final product reflects these shared goals.

- Regular meetings or check-ins can help keep everyone on the same page and provide chances to address issues or changes.

- Clear, descriptive language helps. It is especially useful when avoiding jargon. It can bridge the gap between people with varying expertise.

Navigating Creative Differences

Creative vision differences are common in collaborations. When managed well, they can lead to a more dynamic and innovative final product.

- Approach differences with an open mind. See how other views can add value.

- When conflicts arise, focus on the shared goal: making the best music. Use compromise and negotiation to find agreement.

The Role of the Mixing and Mastering Engineer

The engineer mixes and masters. They act as a mediator between artists and techies. They turn art into sound.

- Understanding the artist's or producer's intent is key. It will help you make informed decisions that improve the track's emotional and sonic impact.

- Clear explanations of technical processes can help show how the processes affect the final sound. This can help nontechnical collaborators understand and allow them to engage with the production process.

Synergy in Sound

Mixing and mastering depend on teamwork, which uses the strengths and visions of everyone involved. The goal is to make a product that is greater than its parts. Teamwork is key for making a harmonious and impactful music project, ensuring that the final mix and master sound pro, and helping the final mix and master fit the team's collaborative spirit.

Troubleshooting Common Mixing and Mastering Issues

In mixing and mastering, audio engineers and producers face many challenges that impact their work's quality. This chapter addresses common issues and challenges that happen during mixing and mastering and gives guidance on how to troubleshoot and fix them.

Muddy Mixes and Lack of Clarity

One of the most common problems in mixing is a muddy sound, where the mix lacks definition and clarity. This often happens because of too much low-frequency energy or from overlapping frequencies from different instruments. To counteract this, it's crucial to use high-pass filtering carefully, which removes unneeded low-end sounds from tracks that don't need them. Strategic EQ can help make space for each element to ensure they fit together like a sonic puzzle.

Harshness and Frequency Imbalance

Harshness in the high frequencies can make a mix tiring to listen to and detract from its overall impact. The mix sounds harsh or unbalanced. To fix this, reduce the levels of bad high frequencies. Also, use de-essing techniques on sibilant vocals or instruments. This will make a smoother, nicer sound. Balancing all mix elements across the frequency spectrum is key to making a smooth and fun listening experience.

Dynamic Range Issues

A mix with too much or too little dynamic range can also pose challenges. Over-compression can lead to a lifeless sound. Too little compression can make a mix lack punch and cohesion. Finding the right balance of compression and limiting is key. This keeps the mix vital and ensures it has a strong, steady sound.

Phase and Stereo Imaging Problems

Phase issues can make parts of a mix lose their impact or vanish. This happens when the mix is summed to mono. Checking the mix in mono and making adjustments to the phase alignment of tracks can prevent these issues. Additionally, improper use of stereo widening effects can lead to a mix that feels disjointed or unstable. Using stereo imaging tools carefully will improve the mix's space and won't hurt its integrity.

Mastering Challenges

Mastering has challenges. These include achieving consistent loudness across tracks, ensuring continuity from track to track, and preparing masters for different formats. You need to use reference tracks, loudness metering, and critical listening. These are crucial for making a master that sounds balanced and cohesive and making sure it sounds good on many playback systems and media formats.

The Role of Critical Listening

At the core of troubleshooting in mixing and mastering is the development of critical listening skills. The ability to identify and rectify issues relies on an engineer's or producer's finely tuned ears. Regularly practice critical listening. Do this in different places and on various sound systems. It will improve your ability to detect and fix audio challenges well.

Problem-Solving in the Studio

Mixing and mastering are as much about problem-solving as they are about creativity. By learning to fix issues and understanding common pitfalls, engineers and producers can avoid unnecessary problems with audio production. They can then create music with confidence and skill to ensure their mixes and masters meet or beat pro standards.

Tips for Efficient Workflow and Time Management

In music production, the world is demanding. Achieving a good workflow and applying time management are key to helping you meet deadlines and keep creative momentum. This chapter offers insights into improving your mixing and mastering workflow to boost productivity without hurting quality.

Setting Up for Success

The foundation of an efficient workflow is a well-organized workspace. A clean, ergonomic setup with easily accessible tools and resources can save time. An organized workspace can cut time wasted searching for files or adjusting settings. Creating templates for various project types can also streamline the setup and let you dive straight into the creative work.

Prioritizing Tasks and Setting Goals

Effective time management starts with clear goal-setting. Breaking down mixing and mastering into tasks helps. The tasks should have objectives and deadlines. This setup keeps focus and momentum. Prioritize these tasks based on their impact on the project to ensure that critical parts get the attention they need.

Harnessing Technology

Using your DAW and other software tools fully can greatly improve workflow. Learning keyboard shortcuts saves time. Using batch processing for repetitive tasks and automation for dynamic changes are also ways to save time. They reduce manual effort.

Avoiding Over-Processing

One common time sink in mixing and mastering is the tendency to over-process tracks. Trusting your ears and making decisive moves can prevent endless tweaking. Setting limits on the number of revisions or steps encourages thoughtful decisions and encourages you to be more deliberate.

Regular Breaks and Listening Sessions

Take regular breaks during long sessions to prevent ear fatigue and keep a fresh perspective on the project. Listen critically sometimes. Do it in different environments and with different equipment, like headphones, car stereos, or other speakers. This can give new insights and stop the need for big last-minute changes.

Learning from Each Project

You will develop time management and workflow skills over time and with experience. Reflect on each project. See what worked well and what could be improved to refine your process for future work. Keeping notes or a project diary can be valuable to capturing lessons and tracking progress over time.

Maximizing Productivity in Music Production

Use these strategies. They will help you make a more structured and focused approach to mixing and mastering. This will lead to higher quality and more satisfaction in your work and give you more time for creativity and innovation in your projects.

Balancing Technical Skill with Creative Expression

Mixing and mastering are fields where technical skill meets creative vision. This chapter covers the balance between the technical and creative sides of audio production. The creative side is fueled by intuition.

Understanding the Technical Foundation

Technical skills are used in mixing and mastering. They provide the framework for creative decisions. You need deep understanding of sound theory. You also need audio processing tools and the technical details of music production. This knowledge ensures that choices during mixing and mastering are informed and effective and make the music better.

Technical skills are crucial. They should serve as tools, not hinder creative vision. Cultivating an environment where creative intuition can flourish is vital. This means allowing for experimentation and taking risks in the mix or master. You must push beyond normal limits to find unique sounds and textures.

The challenge is to strike a balance between technical precision and creative exploration. Focusing too much on perfect technique can lead to sterile, lifeless tracks. But focusing too much on creativity without technique can lead to chaotic, unpolished mixes. Finding a middle ground is key, where technical expertise supports and enhances the creative intent.

Embracing Experimentation and Learning

It is important to balance skill with creativity. This requires a willingness to experiment and always be learning. Each project offers chances to try new techniques, tools, and concepts to build skills and a nuanced approach to music production.

The Role of Collaboration

Working with other artists and producers can also be fertile. It's a good place to balance tech and creativity, and it can introduce new views and ideas. Others challenge your usual ways of thinking and blend technical and creative methods with your own.

Keeping the Listener in Mind

In the end, mixing and mastering aim to create music. The music should connect with listeners. Balancing technical skill with creative expression should improve the listeners' experience. It will make the music more engaging, emotive, and memorable. Keep the end listener in mind. This can guide decisions through production and ensures that the tech and creative parts serve the music's impact.

The Art and Science of Music Production

Balancing technical skill with creative expression is a dynamic process. It is essential for the growth and evolution of a music producer, inspiring a holistic approach to mixing and mastering. In this approach, skill and creativity work together to make compelling, rich music. By embracing both aspects, producers can achieve a more fulfilling and impactful musical journey.

Finding Your Unique Style in Mixing and Mastering

Developing a unique style in mixing and mastering sets great engineers and producers apart. That is what matters in the music industry. This chapter explores how to create a personal sound to make your work recognizable and sought after. Let's transform technical skills into an art.

The Journey to Individuality

Knowing your musical influences and preferences is the first step in defining your unique style. Think about the music that inspires you. Consider how these influences shape how you approach sound.

Experimentation is key. Trying different techniques and approaches can help you find your preferences and strengths.

Learning from the Masters

Study the work of famous mixing and mastering engineers. They are known for their distinctive styles. Analyzing their techniques and understanding their decision-making processes can provide valuable insights. However, the goal is not to copy. It is to learn and adapt these influences. You should use them to create something that is uniquely yours.

Balancing Technicality and Creativity

You need technical skill. But it's the creative use of these skills that defines your style. Develop a mindset that views mixing and mastering not just as tasks to be completed but as opportunities for creative expression. Try unconventional techniques. Don't fear to break the rules. Do it to make a sound that matches your vision.

Establishing a Sonic Signature

Your sonic signature could be how you EQ drums. It could be a reverb setting you often use or an approach to dynamic range. This signature becomes part of your brand, something that clients and listeners begin to recognize and seek.

Feedback and Evolution

Regularly seek feedback from peers, mentors, and clients. Do this to understand how they see your work. Be open to constructive criticism, as it can provide new perspectives and encourage growth. Your style should change over time as you gain experience and learn new techniques. It will also happen as you respond to changes in musical trends and technology.

Marketing Your Unique Sound

Once you've established your style, add it to your personal branding and marketing. Show your unique approach in your portfolio, on your website, and in talks with potential clients. Being able to articulate what sets you apart is crucial in building a reputation in the competitive field of music production.

Your Sound, Your Signature

Finding your unique style in mixing and mastering is a journey. It involves personal and professional growth. It involves a balance of technical skill, creative exploration, and self-reflection. By creating a unique sound, you boost your satisfaction in your work. You also build a brand that can stand out in the music industry. Your unique style will pave the way for a rewarding music production career.

Building Your Portfolio and Brand as a Mixing and Mastering Engineer

The music industry is competitive. Mixing and mastering engineers must build a strong portfolio and brand. These are essential for establishing and growing their careers. This chapter discusses strategies for showing your skills. It covers attracting clients and building a standout reputation.

Crafting a Compelling Portfolio

Your portfolio is the cornerstone of your professional identity. It shows your skills, style, and range.

- Show diversity. Include many types of work in your portfolio. This shows that you can do many different kinds of projects.

- Feature your best work prominently. Show off projects where your mixing and mastering skills had a big impact.

- Give context. Explain the background for each project. Detail your role, the challenges, and how you overcame the challenges to get the result.

Developing Your Brand

Your brand is how the world perceives you and your services. It's your professional identity. It's your values. It's how you talk with the industry.

- Define your brand identity. Figure out what sets you apart from others. Build your brand around your unique strengths and specialties.

- Have consistent messaging. Make sure your communication, from your website to social media, reflects your brand's identity and values.

- Have a professional website and social media profiles. Potential clients can learn about your services, see your work, and contact you.

Networking and Visibility

Building a network within the industry is crucial for growth and success.

- Engage with the community. Attend industry events, workshops, and seminars to connect with potential clients and peers.

- Use online platforms like LinkedIn, Twitter, and industry forums to engage with other professionals and share your expertise.

- Collaborate and partner. Working with other pros can grow your network and open new opportunities.

Marketing and Promotion

Effective marketing can elevate your brand and attract more clients.

- Engage in content marketing. Share your knowledge and experiences through blogs, videos, or podcasts to establish you as an authority in your field.

- Client testimonials showcase positive feedback. They are endorsements from past clients, and they build trust with potential new clients.

- Consider online advertising. It should target your desired clientele. Focus on platforms where they are most likely to engage.

Maintaining Professional Relationships

Your brand's long-term success depends on getting clients and keeping good relationships with them.

- Follow up and keep in touch with past clients. This fosters long-term relationships and encourages repeat business.

- Deliver consistent quality. Doing so will keep up your professional reputation. It will also lead to referrals and repeat work.

Your Brand as Your Legacy

You must build your portfolio and brand as a mixing and mastering engineer. This is an ongoing process requiring clarity of purpose, strategic planning, and consistent effort. By showing your skills and engaging with the industry, you can establish a brand. Do this by delivering exceptional quality. This brand will not only attract clients but also set the stage for a lasting and successful music career.

Networking and Collaboration Opportunities in the Music Industry

Networking and collaboration are vital in the music industry. They are often the lifeline of your career as a mixing and mastering engineer. This chapter explores ways to build meaningful connections. It also covers partnering with others to improve your career and expanding your creative horizons.

Cultivating Professional Relationships

Building a strong network in the music industry is about growing relationships. The relationships are both professional and mutual. Networking involves connecting with many people including fellow engineers and producers, artists, record label executives, and music business pros.

- Engaging with peers at industry events, workshops, and seminars is a great way to start. These gatherings provide opportunities to meet individuals who share your interests and ambitions.
- You can join online forums, social media groups, and webinars to expand your network. This lets you go beyond geography to access a global music professionals community.

The Art of Collaboration

Collaboration is a powerful tool for growth and innovation. It offers chances to learn, create, and explore new musical lands.

- Working with other engineers and producers can open your mind up to new techniques and viewpoints. This will enhance your skills and creativity.

- Working with artists and bands diversifies your portfolio and lets you contribute to music creation, which can lead to long-term partnerships.

Nurturing Your Network

The relationships you build should be nurtured with care and professionalism. Communicating regularly, sharing knowledge, and offering support can strengthen these connections. This will also keep you top of mind for future projects.

- Follow up with contacts often. Do this even when you don't need anything specific. It helps to keep a real and supportive network.

- Share your achievements, updates, and insights in a way that adds value to your network. This will foster a sense of community and collaboration.

Leveraging Technology for Networking

Today's digital age relies on technology, playing a crucial role in networking and collaboration.

- Use sites like LinkedIn, Future Producers, and IllMuzik to connect with industry pros, share your work, and find new jobs.
- You can use digital collaboration tools and cloud platforms to let you work with people from around the world. These tools break down the barriers of physical distance.

But they have their challenges. These include competition, different visions, and logistics.

- Approach each interaction with openness, respect, and a willingness to compromise. Be willing to find common ground.
- Be proactive in preventing conflicts. Use clear communication to avoid misunderstandings and to foster positive relationships.

A Networked Path to Success

Networking and collaboration can greatly impact your music career. Talking with others and building lasting relationships unlocks opportunities for growth, learning, and creativity. Networking and collaboration can help you build a thriving career in mixing and mastering.

Staying Inspired and Continuing Your Education in Mixing and Mastering

The field of music production is ever-evolving. Staying inspired and always learning are key. They keep you relevant and innovative. This chapter discusses strategies for keeping your passion alive and ensuring your skills in mixing and mastering stay at the cutting edge.

Embracing Lifelong Learning

The world of music technology and production methods is always changing. Staying informed is crucial. Continuous learning enhances your technical abilities. It also keeps you creative.

- Formal education can help. You can take advanced courses or get certifications from good music production schools. This will deepen your skills and knowledge.
- Online resources are rich. They include tutorials, webinars, and courses. You can find them on platforms like YouTube, Coursera, and Udemy. Use them to stay updated on the latest trends and techniques.

Seeking Inspiration

Inspiration is the fuel that drives creativity. To keep your work fresh, you need regular doses of inspiration. Get them from many sources.

- Listen to a wide range of music genres and styles. Do this to gain new perspectives and ideas that you can apply to your work.
- Collaboration—working with other creatives—can introduce you to new techniques and

approaches to provide fresh inspiration and chances to learn.

Networking and Community Engagement

Being part of a community of similar professionals can provide support. It can also provide motivation and inspiration. Engaging with your peers can lead to new insights and opportunities for growth.

- Attend conferences, workshops, and seminars to network with peers. You can also learn from industry leaders and stay up to date on trends.
- Join online forums and social media groups for audio engineering and music production to share ideas and experiences.

Balancing Work with Personal Growth

Balancing work and personal growth is important. It's key for long-term success and well-being.

- Manage your time well. Set aside time for self-education and creative experimentation. Do this apart from your routine work. It will keep your skills sharp and your passion alive.

- Practice wellness and mindfulness, which support mental and physical well-being. This will help you stay creative and motivated.

Staying Adaptive and Open to Change

Adapting to new technologies, workflows, and industry shifts is key in the dynamic field of mixing and mastering.

- Embrace new technology. Stay open to using new software, hardware, and methods that can enhance your work and efficiency.

- Have a growth mindset. See challenges as chances to learn and grow, not as obstacles.

A Journey of Continuous Improvement

Staying inspired and continuing your education in mixing and mastering are not just for work but also for sustaining your passion and curiosity. Embrace lifelong learning. Seek new inspiration. Engage with the community. This will ensure a fulfilling and dynamic music production career that constantly evolves with the industry and lets you hone your craft to its highest potential.

The Future of Mixing and Mastering Technology

Audio production is always changing. Technology is shaping the future of mixing and mastering. This chapter explores new trends, tools, and techniques that will redefine the industry and offers insights into how you can stay ahead and use these innovations in your work.

Technological Advancements in Audio Processing

Recent years have seen big advances in digital audio processing. New software and hardware offer unmatched capabilities.

- Artificial intelligence (AI) is being integrated into mixing and mastering software. It provides smart recommendations, automates routine tasks, and offers automated mixing and mastering. These tools can boost efficiency. But they also lead to questions about human creativity and expertise in music.
- Spatial audio and 3D sound are rising in popularity. This is due to the rise of virtual reality and immersive media. Understanding and mastering these technologies will be crucial. Audio engineers will need to master the technology to work in these growing fields.

The Impact of High-Resolution Audio

The demand for high-resolution audio formats is growing. Listeners want the highest quality sound. This trend is pushing engineers to adopt workflows. They must master techniques that keep audio quality. They must meet the strict standards of high-res platforms.

- Recording and mastering now use higher sampling rates. They also use higher bit depths.

This requires adjustments. It demands more from both hardware and software for processing and storage.

- Streaming services offer more lossless and high-resolution audio options. Mastering for these formats needs careful thought. Dynamics, frequency, and encoding must be considered.

Cloud-Based Collaboration and Production

Cloud technology is revolutionizing the way audio professionals collaborate and produce music.

- Cloud platforms allow real-time collaboration across different locations. They make it easier to work on projects with clients and colleagues around the world.

- New tech is paving the way for fully virtual studios. Mixing and mastering can be done in the cloud. This offers flexibility and scalability.

Preparing for the Future

To stay relevant in audio production, you need to keep learning. The field is changing fast.

- Keeping abreast of new technologies is key. Regularly update your knowledge and skills to include the latest software and hardware. This will ensure you stay competitive.
- Try new techniques. Being open to new techniques can lead to new sounds and styles, setting your work apart.

Embracing Change in Audio Production

The future of mixing and mastering technology is full of exciting possibilities. But it also has challenges. Stay informed about the latest trends and developments. Embrace new technologies and adapt your skills so you can navigate future audio production with confidence and creativity. You've been given a glimpse into the future, and we encourage you to be an active part in shaping it. You should use these advances to improve your work and impact the industry.

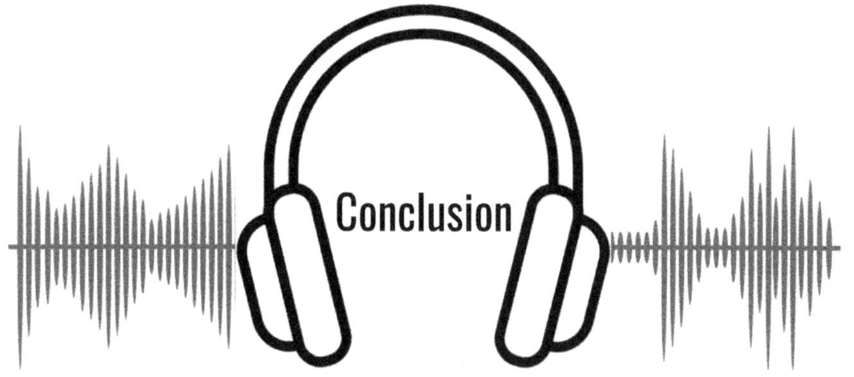

Your Journey to Mastery Begins Here

As we reach the end of this guide, it's time to think about the journey through the complex world of mixing and mastering. You must start with understanding the basics, then you can explore advanced techniques and future trends. The path to mastery is hard but rewarding.

Mixing and mastering are arts that continually evolve with technology and trends. Mastery is not a destination. It's a path of learning, experimentation, and growth. Embracing this process is key to staying relevant and innovative in music production, which is a dynamic field.

Applying Knowledge to Practice

You can now use the knowledge and insights found in this book in the studio. That's where theory meets practice. Each project you take is a chance to improve your skills. You can also develop your style and add something unique to the music.

Building a Network of Creativity and Support

Remember the importance of networking and collaboration in your career. Building relationships with other professionals can lead to new opportunities and bring shared knowledge and a support system that fosters creativity and growth.

Staying Inspired and Motivated

You must keep your passion for music and sound. It is key for having a fulfilling career in mixing and mastering. Stay inspired by always seeking new sources of creativity. These can be found in music, nature, technology, or collaboration with others.

Preparing for the Future

The future of mixing and mastering is exciting and full of possibilities. Stay curious and open-minded. Be ready to explore new tech and methods. They can enhance your work and change the industry.

Your Unique Contribution

As you move forward, remember, your unique view and creativity are your best assets. Your technical skills and knowledge are tools to express these qualities. They shape sounds and songs that resonate with listeners and last.

Becoming a master in mixing and mastering is a personal and professional adventure for you. It extends beyond the pages of this book. With dedication, passion, and a love of improvement, you can achieve excellence in your craft. You can also make a lasting impact in the world of music. Let this book be a step on your path to becoming a masterful mixing and mastering engineer, then you will be ready to face the challenges and opportunities ahead with confidence and skill.

Mixing and Mastering Quiz

Take this quiz to test your understanding of the concepts and techniques from this book. Each question corresponds to a specific chapter, providing a focused review of the material.

1. What is the primary goal of mastering in music production?
2. Explain how mixing and mastering contribute to the final presentation of a musical piece.
3. List three pieces of equipment essential for a basic home mixing and mastering studio.
4. Why is acoustic treatment important in a mixing and mastering workspace?
5. Describe the significance of headroom in the mixing process.
6. What is the purpose of using EQ in mixing?

7. How does compression affect the dynamic range of a track?

8. Distinguish the differences between reverb and delay effects.

9. Name one creative effect and describe its impact on a mix.

10. Explain what parallel compression is and how it is used in mixing.

11. What should be the focus when preparing a mix for mastering?

12. Identify a common tool used in mastering and its purpose.

13. How do mastering EQ and compression differ from their mixing counterparts?

14. What is stereo imaging, and why is it important in mastering?

15. Describe a scenario where multiband compression would be used in mastering.

16. What is the purpose of loudness normalization in streaming platforms?
17. Why would a mastering approach differ between vinyl and digital formats?
18. What is the role of sequencing in album mastering?
19. How does effective communication impact the mixing and mastering process?
20. What is a common issue in mixing, and how can it be resolved?
21. Give one tip for maintaining an efficient workflow in music production.
22. Why is it important to balance technical skill with creative expression in audio production?
23. How can an engineer or producer develop a unique style in mixing and mastering?
24. What is one key element in building a successful brand as a mixing/mastering engineer?

25. How can networking benefit a mixing and mastering engineer's career?

26. Why is continuous education important in the field of mixing and mastering?

27. Name one emerging technology that could impact the future of mixing and mastering.

Answers

1. The primary goal of mastering is to ensure the mix is balanced, cohesive, and optimized for various playback systems.

2. Mixing and mastering make sure all track elements are balanced. They also optimize sound to work well in different listening environments.

3. Three essential pieces of equipment for a home studio are a reliable computer, an audio interface, and studio monitors.

4. Acoustic treatment is crucial for accurate hearing. It prevents room acoustics from

coloring the sound, which ensures decisions are based on true sounds.

5. Headroom in mixing is important to avoid digital clipping and to allow space for mastering processes like EQ and compression.

6. EQ is used in mixing to shape the tone of individual tracks, remove unwanted frequencies, and help elements fit better together within a mix.

7. Compression reduces a track's dynamic range. It makes loud sounds quieter and quiet sounds louder. This helps to keep a consistent level in the track.

8. Reverb adds a sense of spatial depth and ambiance to sounds, while delay repeats audio signals to create echo effects.

9. A creative effect such as a phaser can add movement and texture to a static pad sound, making it more lively and interesting.

10. Parallel compression, or New York compression, involves mixing a heavily compressed track with the original uncompressed one. This maintains natural dynamics while enhancing power and presence.

11. When preparing a mix for mastering, focus on a clean, dynamic, and balanced mix. Leave enough headroom for the mastering engineer to work well.

12. A limiter is a common tool in mastering. It prevents audio peaks from going over the digital clipping point. This keeps the overall loudness up and stops distortion.

13. You apply EQ and compression more subtly and broadly in mastering. They affect the entire track to make sure it sounds cohesive and polished.

14. Good stereo imaging is crucial in mastering because it creates a wide, enveloping soundstage. This stage enhances the listener's experience without hurting the mix's balance on different systems.

15. In mastering, multiband compression controls the dynamics of specific frequency ranges. It does so independently, allowing for precise shaping without affecting the whole spectrum.

16. Streaming platforms use loudness normalization to make sure all music plays at a consistent volume. This gives listeners a uniform auditory experience.

17. Mastering for vinyl differs from digital formats because vinyl has physical limits, which require careful consideration of dynamics and extreme frequencies.

18. In album mastering, sequencing involves arranging the tracks in a flow. The order tells a story and keeps up the album's energy and emotion.

19. Effective communication ensures all involved parties understand the project goals. This understanding helps in making a final product that meets everyone's expectations and artistic vision.

20. A common mixing issue like muddiness can be resolved by using EQ to cut unnecessary low frequencies and enhance clarity.

21. One tip for maintaining an efficient workflow is to organize and label tracks clearly and use templates to speed up the setup process.

22. Balancing tech skill with creativity is important to ensure that tech aspects of audio enhance, not stifle, the music's creativity.

23. An engineer can develop a unique style by trying new techniques, learning new methods, and using their artistic instincts.

24. A key part of building a successful brand as a mixing/mastering engineer is delivering high-quality work. The work should reflect a unique sound.

25. Networking can introduce engineers to new clients, open up collaboration, and facilitate the sharing of ideas and techniques. These can enhance one's skills and reputation.

26. Continuous education is important in mixing and mastering because it helps you keep up with evolving tech and techniques to ensure you remain competitive and effective in the industry.

27. New technologies like artificial intelligence (AI) in music will impact mixing and mastering by automating routine tasks and offering new ways to analyze and improve sound.

Resources

The journey of understanding mixing and mastering requires many resources that can provide guidance, inspiration, and technical support. Here's a curated list of resources that can be invaluable to music producers and audio engineers.

Books

1. *The Mixing Engineer's Handbook* by Bobby Owsinski is a detailed guide covering every part of mixing. It starts with basic concepts and goes to advanced techniques.

2. *Mastering Audio: The Art and the Science* by Bob Katz is an in-depth exploration of mastering, providing insights into technical processes and artistic choices.

Online Courses and Tutorials

1. Berklee Online offers professional courses that cover mixing, mastering, and music production. They are taught by industry experts.

2. Udemy features a wide range of courses on audio engineering, from beginner to advanced levels.

Software and Plugins

1. Waves Audio is a leading developer of audio plugins for mixing, mastering, and post-production.

2. iZotope is known for its advanced audio processing software, including RX for audio repair and Ozone for mastering.

Forums and Communities

1. Gearspace is an online forum where professionals discuss recording, mixing, mastering, and music production.

2. Reddit (r/audioengineering) is a subreddit dedicated to discussing all parts of audio engineering. This includes mixing and mastering.

YouTube Channels

1. Produce Like A Pro offers tutorials, tips, and interviews. They feature industry pros and cover all parts of music production.

2. Mix with the Masters features masterclass videos from some of the world's leading mix and mastering engineers.

Professional Organizations

1. Audio Engineering Society (AES) is an international organization dedicated to audio engineering. It offers resources, events, and networking.

2. Music Producers Guild (MPG) is a professional body that represents music producers and engineers. It provides networking, advocacy, and educational resources.

Reference Materials and Tools

1. Sonic Visualiser is an app for viewing and analyzing audio files. It is useful for education and research.

2. Tunebat is a tool for music producers to analyze and match the key, tempo, and other elements of music tracks.

Other Resources

Research Papers and Articles: Scholarly articles on audio processing, psychoacoustics, and music technology can provide scientific insights into the sound engineering principles.

Interviews and Case Studies: Insights from experienced music producers and audio engineers, as featured in magazines, like *Sound on Sound* or *Mix*, can provide practical and real-world perspectives.

Software Manuals: Detailed guides and manuals from DAWs and audio processing software can provide specific information on tools and techniques used in mixing and mastering.

Glossary

This glossary provides a quick reference to key terms used throughout the book, helping readers understand the technical language associated with mixing and mastering in music production.

A

- Amplitude: The height of a sound wave, representing the volume or loudness of a sound.
- Attack: The time it takes for a compressor to begin reducing the level of the signal once it exceeds the threshold.

B

- Bass Traps: Acoustic absorbers designed to catch low-frequency sounds, reducing bass buildup in a room.

C

- Compression: A process that reduces the dynamic range of an audio signal, making loud sounds quieter and quiet sounds louder.

- Crossfade: A technique used to blend two sounds or tracks, where one fades out while the other fades in.

D

- DAW (Digital Audio Workstation): A software application used for recording, editing, mixing, and mastering audio.
- Decay: The time it takes for a sound to fade away after the initial attack.

E

- EQ (Equalization): The process of adjusting the balance of frequency components within an audio signal.
- Exciter: An audio effect that enhances the harmonics of a sound, adding clarity and perceived brightness.

F

- Frequency: The number of times a sound wave cycles per second, measured in hertz (Hz), determining the pitch of the sound.

G

- Gain Staging: The process of managing the levels of audio signals within the recording and mixing process to prevent distortion and noise.

H

- Headroom: The amount of available dynamic range in an audio signal before it reaches the maximum level and distorts.

I

- Imaging: The perceived spatial locations of sound sources in stereo or surround sound, including width, depth, and height.

L

- Limiting: A type of compression with a very high ratio used to ensure that the audio signal does not exceed a certain level.
- LUFS (Loudness Units Full Scale): A standard measurement of audio loudness that aims to normalize perceived volume levels across different audio sources.

M

- Mastering: The final process of audio post-production, which involves optimizing the final mix's frequency balance, dynamics, and loudness.
- Mid-side Processing: A stereo recording and mixing technique that separates audio into mid (center) and side (left and right) components for independent processing.

P

- Panning: The distribution of a sound signal in a stereo or multi-channel sound field, used to create a sense of location or movement.
- Phantom Center: The perceived center point in stereo sound, created by an equal audio signal in the left and right speakers.

R

- Reverb (Reverberation): The persistence of sound after the sound source has been stopped, created by reflections from surfaces in an environment.

S

- Sampling Rate: The number of samples of audio carried per second, measured in hertz (Hz).
- Stereo Width: The perceived spatial extent of the sound field in stereo recordings, ranging from narrow (mono) to wide (full stereo).

T

- Threshold: The level at which a processor like a compressor or limiter begins to affect the audio signal.
- Transient: A short-duration high-amplitude sound at the beginning of a waveform, like a drum hit or plucked string.

W

- Wct/Dry Mix: A control on an effects processor that blends the unprocessed (dry) signal with the processed (wet) signal.

Thank You for Embarking on This Sonic Journey

As you turn the final page of this guide, we thank you. We thank you for letting Slime Green Beats join you on your voyage through mixing and mastering.

The path to mastering your sound is a lifelong endeavor. It is full of challenges, learning, and growth. We hope this book gave you valuable insights and practical knowledge. Most importantly, we hope it inspired you. Keep pushing the limits of what you can achieve in music.

Remember, the end of this book is not the conclusion of your journey but a new beginning. You've acquired tools and techniques. With them, your mixing and mastering adventures are set to reach new heights. We look forward to hearing your amazing music. We also can't wait to see the impact you will have in the sonic universe.

Thank you for reading, and may your passion for music continue to grow and resonate in every beat you craft.

Keep mixing, keep mastering, and keep inspiring!

—Slime Green Beats and the Team

Visit Slime Green Beats online for more resources and inspiration:

- Free Melody Loops Pack: https://slimegreenbeats.com/products/free-melody-loops-pack
- Beats for Sale: https://slimegreenbeats.com/pages/beats-for-sale
- Music Production Blog: https://slimegreenbeats.com/blogs/music

www.ingramcontent.com/pod-product-compliance
Lightning Source LLC
LaVergne TN
LVHW010946110826
845149LV00015B/3236

* 9 7 9 8 9 9 0 7 8 1 5 4 2 *